Go, Critter, Go!

Spin, Spider, Spin!

Dana Meachen Rau

Marshall Cavendish
Benchmark
New York

Spiders have eight legs.

Spiders have eight eyes.

Spiders live in grass.

Spiders live in trees.

Spiders make silk.

Spiders spin webs.

13

Spiders catch bugs.

Spiders eat bugs.

Spin, spider, spin!

19

Words We Know

bug

eyes

grass

legs

silk

tree

web

Index

Page numbers in **boldface** are illustrations.

About the Author

Dana Meachen Rau is an author, editor, and illustrator. A graduate of Trinity College in Hartford, Connecticut, she has written more than one hundred fifty books for children, including nonfiction, biographies, early readers, and historical fiction. She lives with her family in Burlington, Connecticut.

With thanks to the Reading Consultants:

Nanci Vargus, Ed.D., is an Assistant Professor of Elementary Education at the University of Indianapolis.

Beth Walker Gambro received her M.S. Ed. Reading from the University of St. Francis, Joliet, Illinois.

Marshall Cavendish Benchmark
99 White Plains Road
Tarrytown, New York 10591-9001
www.marshallcavendish.us

Library of Congress Cataloging-in-Publication Data

Rau, Dana Meachen, 1971–
Spin, spider, spin! / by Dana Meachen Rau.
p. cm. — (Bookworms. Go, critter, go!)
Summary: "Describes characteristics and behaviors of spiders"—Provided by publisher.
Includes index.
ISBN-13: 978-0-7614-2653-0
1. Spiders—Juvenile literature. I. Title. II. Series.
QL458.4.R38 2007
595.4'4—dc22
2006034225

Editor: Christina Gardeski
Publisher: Michelle Bisson
Designer: Virginia Pope
Art Director: Anahid Hamparian

Photo Research by Anne Burns Images

Cover Photo by *Animals Animals*/Maresa Pryor

The photographs in this book are used with permission and through the courtesy of:
Animals Animals: pp. 1, 19 Bill Beatty; pp. 5, 20TR James Robinson; pp. 11, 21TL Ralph Reinhold;
p. 15 Carson Baldwin, Jr. *Corbis*: pp. 3, 20BR Michael Maconachie; pp. 7, 20BL Dennis Johnson/Papilio;
pp. 9, 21TR Ian Beames/Ecoscene; pp. 3, 21B Wolfgang Kaehler. *Peter Arnold*: pp. 17, 20TL BIOS/Bricout.

Printed in Malaysia
1 3 5 6 4 2